PUERTO RICO

Past and Present

Maria DaSilva-Gordon

rosen publishing's
rosen central

New York

Dedicated to my husband, who encourages and supports my passion for exploring new places (even if he can't always come along). To my family and friends, thank you for your love and support.

Published in 2011 by The Rosen Publishing Group, Inc.
29 East 21st Street, New York, NY 10010

First Edition

Library of Congress Cataloging-in-Publication Data

DaSilva-Gordon, Maria.
Puerto Rico: past and present / Maria DaSilva-Gordon.—1st ed.
    p. cm.—(The United States: Past and present)
Includes bibliographical references and index.
ISBN 978-1-4358-9502-7 (library binding)
ISBN 978-1-4358-9529-4 (pbk.)
ISBN 978-1-4358-9563-8 (6-pack)
1. Puerto Rico—Juvenile literature. I. Title.
F1958.3.D37 2011
972.95—dc22

2010005891

Manufactured in Malaysia

CPSIA Compliance Information: Batch #S10YA: For further information, contact Rosen Publishing, New York, New York, at 1-800-237-9932.

On the cover: Top left: Locals cut and gather sugarcane stalks in the 1960s. Top right: Puerto Rico is known for its relaxing environment. Bottom: Rainforests and waterfalls are some of Puerto Rico's natural attractions.

Contents

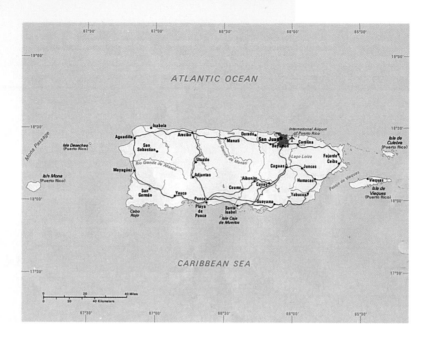

Located in the Caribbean, Puerto Rico is about 1,280 miles (2,060 kilometers) from the Florida coast. Puerto Rico is made up of a main island and several smaller islands.

Introduction

Puerto Rico is an island in the Caribbean that came under U.S. rule in 1898. From soaring mountains to bays that glow to stunning beaches, Puerto Rico's land offers variety. The island is home to tropical rainforests, large systems of caves, and roaring waterfalls. There are also numerous types of trees, flowers, and plants in Puerto Rico.

The people who live on the island are just as diverse as the land. Puerto Rico is a mix of cultural influences—Taíno, African, Spanish, and American. This melting pot of cultures is the result of Puerto Rico's history, which featured explorers, invaders, and slaves. Today, Puerto Rico's history lives on in the traditions of its people.

Minus a brief period of time, the Puerto Rico discovered by Christopher Columbus has never known independence. Spain ruled for four hundred years, and then the United States took control.

Today, Puerto Rico has more control over its own affairs than it did when the United States first took over. However, it is still strongly linked to America. The banking and postal systems used in Puerto Rico are within the U.S. system. The currency is the U.S. dollar. Puerto Rico is an unincorporated U.S. territory, and Puerto Ricans are considered U.S. citizens. No visas or passports are required to enter Puerto Rico from the United States or vice versa. English and Spanish are the official languages.

Even though Puerto Rico is not connected to the United States by land, it is still an important and unique part of the country.

Chapter 1

THE GEOGRAPHY OF PUERTO RICO

Puerto Rico is situated in the Caribbean between North America and South America, about 1,280 miles (2,060 kilometers) from the coast of Florida. It is surrounded by water, with the Atlantic Ocean to its north and the Caribbean Sea to its south. Puerto Rico is part of a chain of islands known as the Greater Antilles, along with Jamaica, Cuba, and Hispaniola. Puerto Rico lies east of Hispaniola, an island shared by the Dominican Republic and Haiti.

Puerto Rico is made up of a main island that is about 110 miles (177 km) from east to west and 35 miles (56 km) from north to south. It takes about three hours to drive between the island's most distant points. Along with the main island, Puerto Rico is made up of several smaller islands and various islets and cays (tiny islands).

Puerto Rico has a mild climate. It does not experience the harsh, cold winters found in North America. Winters, which run roughly from October to early March, have an average temperature of 74 degrees Fahrenheit (23 degrees Celsius) along the coast. In the summers, the average temperature along the coast is about 81°F (27°C). In the mountains, temperatures are typically about 5 to 10°F (3 to 6°C) lower. The average rainfall in Puerto Rico is 70 inches (178 centimeters) per year.

The Cordillera Central features stunning scenery, winding roads, and cooler temperatures. The area is home to the island's deepest gorge, San Cristóbal Canyon, and highest peak, Cerro de Punta.

Terrain

When it comes to the land's physical features, Puerto Rico has a little bit of everything. The three main geographic regions are the mountainous interior, the coastal plains, and the karst region.

Running across the center of the main island, from east to west, is a chain of mountains called the Cordillera Central (the Central Mountain Range). The highest mountain is Cerro de Punta, at 4,393

Hurricanes: A Caribbean Threat

Puerto Rico is situated in a geographic area that is prone to hurricanes. Although the Caribbean hurricane season runs from June to November, the highest chances for hurricanes are in September and October. Hurricanes have been, and continue to be, a part of Puerto Rico's history. The first hurricane to hit following Puerto Rico's colonization by the Spanish occurred in 1515. A second hurricane struck in 1526. In 1530, there were three hurricanes in Puerto Rico within a two-month period.

In the nineteenth and early twentieth centuries, when Puerto Rico was heavily dependent on crops, hurricanes had the potential to greatly affect an entire industry and the island's economy. For example, the San Ciriaco hurricane of 1899 struck the coffee regions in the mountains particularly hard. Coffee plantations were entirely destroyed. In fact, the hurricane contributed to the downfall of the island's coffee economy. The San Ciriaco hurricane also had a negative impact on Puerto Rico's sugar industry. In 1928, the San Felipe hurricane devastated Puerto Rico's fruit industry.

Puerto Rico is still vulnerable to hurricanes and the damages they bring. For instance, in 1998, Hurricane Georges caused more than $1 billion in property destruction. But what happens after a hurricane hits has changed since earlier times.

Today, Puerto Rico is less likely to be devastated economically by crop losses. This is because Puerto Rico is not as dependent on crops as it was in the past. Instead, Puerto Rico relies more on industry, with strong industries in pharmaceuticals (medicines), electronics, and apparel. In addition, when a major hurricane happens, Puerto Rico receives financial help from the United States. When Hurricane Hugo caused serious destruction in 1989, the United States declared Puerto Rico a federal disaster area. This meant that the island received emergency relief money.

feet (1,339 meters). There is a narrow strip of lowlands along the coast, where most of the population lives.

Puerto Rico has karst regions, which include rocky ground, sinkholes, impressive caves, and underground streams. In fact, one system of caves, the Río Camuy Caves, is considered the third largest in the world. Carved over time by the Río Camuy (Camuy River), these caves are found in northwest Puerto Rico in an area that is about 10 miles (16 km) long. Inside the caves are various stalagmites and stalactites. One cave even houses forty-two petroglyphs, or rock carvings. Millions of bats have called these caves home. Also, Mona Island—one of Puerto Rico's smaller islands—has about twenty limestone caves.

Puerto Rico is also home to different kinds of forests. El Yunque National Forest in the east is an estimated 28,000 acres (11,331 hectares) of tropical rainforest. Coastal dry forest can be found in the northeast in Las Cabezas de San Juan Nature Reserve and in the southwest in the Guánica Biosphere Reserve and Forest. Guajataca State Forest is 2,300 acres (931 ha) of subtropical rainforest in the northwest. Situated in the karst region, the terrain here ranges from 500 to 1,000 feet (152 to 305 m) above sea level.

Islands

Along with the main island, there are a number of smaller islands and islets that make up Puerto Rico. The three largest are Mona Island, Culebra Island, and Vieques Island. Mona Island is located about 50 miles (80 km) off the west coast of the mainland. It is about 20 square miles (52 sq km) in area. The nearly circular island has been uninhabited for more than fifty years. It has been a nature reserve for ninety years. Mona Island is home to many iguanas, turtles, and seabirds.

Culebra Island is located about 17 miles (27 km) east of the mainland. The island is just 7 miles (11 km) long and 3 miles (5 km) wide and has a total land area of 7,000 acres (2,833 ha). Of that area, more than 1,500 acres (607 ha) make up the Culebra National Wildlife Refuge. About two thousand people live on Culebra.

South of Culebra and larger in size is Vieques, which is about 7 miles (11 km) east of the main island. Vieques measures about 21 miles (34 km) long and 4 miles (6.4 km) wide and comprises about 33,000 acres (13,355 ha) in area. Once the site of a U.S. naval base, the island is now home to the largest national wildlife refuge in the Caribbean, the Vieques National Wildlife Refuge, with 17,771 acres (7,192 ha). Vieques has a population of almost ten thousand people.

Water

Puerto Rico is just as diverse when it comes to its bodies of water. Several bays in Puerto Rico glow green, thanks to bioluminescent microorganisms that reside in the water. Throughout the world, there are seven known bodies of water that do this. Puerto Rico, which is home to three of them, is considered to have the brightest spots. One example is Bioluminescent Bay, a lagoon on the island of Vieques. Waterfalls can also be found in Puerto Rico. The island's tallest is about 500 feet (152 m) and is near the Central Mountain town of Aibonito.

Puerto Rico is also known for its mangrove bays, which are made up of tropical evergreen trees and shrubs that cluster along tidal shores. Located on the southern coastline, the National Estuarine Research Reserve is the island's largest mangrove estuary. There are also several lagoons in Puerto Rico, such as the saltwater lagoon

At night, visitors to Puerto Rico take to the waters in search of an unusual sight: bioluminescent microorganisms. They cause some of the islands' bodies of water to glow green.

The colorful and endangered Puerto Rican parrot is one of more than 250 species of birds found on the island. Many places in Puerto Rico are ideal for bird-watching.

found in the Reserva Natural Laguna de Joyuda on the west coast of the main island.

Puerto Rico only has one natural lake, Laguna Tortuguero, which is found on the north coast. Puerto Rico has a number of rivers that flow from the island's interior to the north and west coasts. These rivers include the Grande de Arecibo, Grande de Añasco, La Plata, Cibuco, Grande de Loíza, and Bayamón.

Animal and Plant Life

Puerto Rico offers a range of animal and plant life. Among the animals that inhabit the island are wild horses, mongooses, monkeys, and bats. Aquatic mammals include the humpback whale, dolphin, and manatee. Sixty-one species of reptiles and twenty-five species of amphibians inhabit the island. With its distinct and loud chirping call, the coquí frog is one of Puerto Rico's well-known amphibians.

Tanagers, herons, ospreys, warblers, and brown pelicans are some of the more than 250 species of birds found in Puerto Rico. The endangered yellow-shouldered blackbird and Puerto Rican parrot also live in the area.

The types of saltwater fish in Puerto Rico include shellfish, snapper, mahi-mahi, shark, tuna, and blue and white marlin. Puerto Rico hosts the International Billfish Tournament, one of the oldest big-game fishing tournaments worldwide. In addition, more than 240 species of fish live in Puerto Rico's coral reefs, and a number of freshwater species live in the rivers and streams.

Only found in Puerto Rico, the coquí is famous for its sound. Although tiny in size, this tree frog has a loud, chirping call that can be heard at night.

Tree varieties include mangroves, blue mahoe trees, fruit-bearing trees, and ceibas. Even cacti can be found in Puerto Rico. While flora decorates homes throughout the island, some of the best places to examine the island's plant life are in state parks. For instance, El Yunque National Forest boasts fifty types of ferns and more than twenty varieties of orchids. About 240 types of trees are also located in El Yunque.

Chapter 2

THE HISTORY OF PUERTO RICO

In 1493, Christopher Columbus arrived in Puerto Rico. There, he encountered the Taíno, a Native American group living on the island. Fifteen years later, in 1508, Juan Ponce de León returned with fifty soldiers to colonize the island on behalf of Spain. For the next four hundred years, the Spanish ruled Puerto Rico. During this time, the island experienced its share of attempted invasions. From the 1500s through the end of the 1700s, Puerto Rico was attacked by those in search of gold and land.

For the most part, the Spaniards were successful in fighting off these attacks. Two Spanish-built forts played a part in the defense of the island. The first, El Morro, was built to fend off any attacks by sea. Later, Castillo de San Cristóbal (Fort St. Christopher) was added to protect against invasions by land. Both forts are in the city of San Juan.

Invasions

Puerto Rico was an important location for Spain to control. By holding Puerto Rico, Spain could guard its valuable treasure ships returning from Mexico and South America. Spain also had a base for protecting its other colonies in the New World.

Built starting in the 1500s, El Morro helped fend off attacks by sea. A World Heritage Site, the fort contains six levels, including dungeons, lookouts, secret access tunnels, and artillery posts.

Because of its desirable location, many rival nations tried to take over Puerto Rico. Between 1528 and 1554, French privateers mounted a number of attacks in Puerto Rico. While they succeeded in destroying the town of San Germán (on several different occasions), the French never gained command of the island.

In 1595, the English took a turn at invading Puerto Rico when Sir Francis Drake arrived. Drake came in search of a Spanish galleon carrying about $2 million in gold coins. The Spaniards forced him to retreat, and he left with nothing. Three years later, the British returned with a fleet of twenty ships. Following a short battle, the Spanish surrendered the capital of San Juan and the British moved

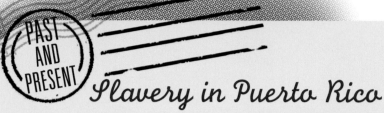

Slavery in Puerto Rico

Like the United States, Puerto Rico has slavery as part of its history. When Puerto Rico was first discovered, the Taíno people were living on the island. The Spanish put this group of native islanders to work mining for gold. At first, the Spanish agreed to pay the Taíno for their labor, but they soon began using them as slaves. In response, the Taíno tried to rebel against the Spanish. During one uprising, they destroyed a town and killed about one hundred Spaniards. The Spanish ended the revolt, and the Taíno never did win their freedom.

As slaves, the Taíno population quickly began to decrease. When the Spanish first colonized the area in 1508, thousands of Taínos lived on the island. Estimates of the Taíno population during this time range from twenty thousand to fifty thousand. Less than a decade later, however, there were about four thousand Taínos living on the island. By 1544, following years of slavery, poor treatment, and the spread of European diseases, the Taíno population in Puerto Rico numbered less than one hundred.

In the 1500s, Africans were brought to the island to replace the Taíno as slaves. By 1531, there were more than 1,500 African slaves in Puerto Rico. By 1830, there were thirty-one thousand. Like the Taíno, Africans were forced to mine for gold. When there was no more gold to mine, Africans were forced to cut sugarcane. Like the Taíno, the African slaves fought for their freedom. In later years, a political movement for freedom began to take shape during a time of wider uprisings against Spain. A Puerto Rican abolitionist living in Spain led this movement, along with political leaders living on the island. Eventually, in 1873, the Spanish National Assembly abolished slavery.

Today, descendants of the Taíno make up just 0.7 percent of the nearly four million people that call Puerto Rico home. Only 11 percent of the population is of African descent. Despite their small representation in Puerto Rico's population, the Taíno and Africans live on in various cultural traditions that have been preserved throughout the island.

in. But the British victory was short-lived: they left Puerto Rico ten weeks later because of a dysentery epidemic.

In 1625, the Dutch attacked Puerto Rico. The Dutch shot more than four thousand cannonballs into San Juan's walls, landed eight hundred men, and occupied the city for about a month. The Spanish, however, were able to hold El Morro. Puerto Rican militiamen fought back against the Dutch, and they retreated. On their way out, the Dutch looted and burned the city. Included in the destruction were almost one hundred houses and San Juan's library.

During the 1700s, there were minor attacks by the English and Dutch. All of them proved unsuccessful. Then, in 1797, the English launched an ambitious attack. The British arrived with more than sixty ships and a force of about seven thousand men. Intense fighting lasted for two weeks before the British retreated.

Fights for Independence

Along with attacks from invaders, the Spanish had to handle uprisings from within Puerto Rico. During the 1800s, there were several efforts by Puerto Ricans to gain independence from Spain. One of the most famous attempts occurred on September 23, 1868. On this date, about six hundred men and women marched on the small, western town of Lares. During this uprising, Puerto Rican protesters briefly took control of the town and named the island the Republic of Puerto Rico. The victory did not last long: within twenty-four hours, the protesters came under heavy Spanish attack. The uprising became known as Grito de Lares, or the Cry of Lares, and September 23 became a national holiday in honor of the revolt.

In time, political parties that supported independence formed in Puerto Rico. The newspaper *La Democracia* published arguments

On September 23 in Lares, Puerto Rican activists in favor of independence celebrate the Grito de Lares, a famous attempt by Puerto Ricans to gain freedom from Spain.

for independence and shined a spotlight on the injustices of Spanish rule. Finally, in 1897, Spain granted Puerto Rico autonomy. Puerto Rico's new government was made official the following year.

The island's independence, however, was brief. By mid-1898, Spain had become involved in a war with America. The Spanish-American War lasted six months and ended with Spain surrendering Puerto Rico to the United States. The island officially came under U.S. control—and the war officially ended—with the signing of the Treaty of Paris on December 10, 1898.

The Twentieth Century

Since the beginning of the twentieth century, Puerto Rico has had some power to govern itself. Its form of self-government began to take shape in 1900, when the U.S. Congress passed the Foraker Act. After two years of U.S. military rule, this act created a civilian government in Puerto Rico. According to the Foraker Act, the president appointed the governor of Puerto Rico, as well as an executive council. Puerto Ricans had the ability to elect the members of one legislative house. In addition, the island's people elected a resident commissioner. The commissioner was able to speak on behalf of Puerto Rico in Congress, but did not have any voting power.

In 1917, the Jones Act granted U.S. citizenship to residents of Puerto Rico. Puerto Ricans who supported independence from the United States were not happy with this act. In the following years, many Puerto Ricans continued to voice their preference for more autonomy from the United States. Their efforts began to pay off. In 1946, the United States appointed the island's first native to the post of governor. In 1948, Puerto Ricans voted for their own governor for the first time. In 1951, Puerto Ricans held a vote to see if the

A Puerto Rican woman stands next to a homemade sign for Luis Muñoz Marín, the first popularly elected governor of Puerto Rico, in 1948.

island would remain a colony or become a commonwealth. Residents voted for a commonwealth. A year later, Puerto Rico's commonwealth status—along with a constitution that was written and approved by residents—was made official. As a commonwealth, the island governs itself, with U.S. supervision.

Today, there continues to be debate regarding Puerto Rico's status. Some people believe that Puerto Rico should have independence from the United States, and others think Puerto Rico should become a U.S. state. There are also those who prefer Puerto Rico to remain the way it is, a commonwealth.

Chapter 3

THE GOVERNMENT OF PUERTO RICO

As residents of a commonwealth, Puerto Ricans can vote in Democratic and Republican primary elections but not in the general election for the U.S. president. The government of the commonwealth is based in San Juan, which is the capital of Puerto Rico. The structure of Puerto Rico's government is very similar to the structure used in the United States. Both the U.S. and Puerto Rico have three branches of government: executive, legislative, and judicial.

Executive Branch

In Puerto Rico, the executive branch is made up of a governor and department secretaries. The governor executes laws and makes government appointments. Some of the governor's appointments require approval from the Puerto Rican legislature. The governor also serves as the commander in chief of the militia.

A person must be at least thirty-five years old to be governor. He or she must also be a U.S. citizen and a resident of Puerto Rico for the five years prior to serving. The citizens of Puerto Rico elect a governor during general elections. If elected, the governor serves for four years. A governor can be reelected and can serve an unlimited number of terms.

Like the governor, the department secretaries are part of Puerto Rico's executive branch of government. Department secretaries are appointed by the governor with the senate's approval. The secretaries form an advisory council to the governor. If the governor can no longer perform his or her duties, one of the department secretaries— the secretary of state—takes over the governor's job.

Once a fortress, La Fortaleza is now used as the official residence and offices of Puerto Rico's governor. It is the oldest executive mansion in continuous use in the Western Hemisphere.

Legislative Branch

The legislative branch operates as a bicameral, or two-part, system. Responsibilities of this governmental branch include introducing bills and passing them into law, conducting studies and investigations, and letting citizens know about public business. Members of the legislative branch are elected by direct vote in general elections. If elected, members serve four-year terms.

The House of Representatives of Puerto Rico is one part, or chamber, of the legislative branch. The number of representatives can vary, but there are normally fifty-one. The house is made up of forty district members, one for each of Puerto Rico's forty representative districts. There are also at least eleven members at large.

Puerto Rico's Government

Puerto Rico's government has undergone many changes during its history. With the Charter of Autonomy of 1897, Puerto Rico became an independent state under a Spanish governor. The island also received representation in the Spanish parliament. Two chambers were created: a council of administration, made up mostly of elected members, and a house of representatives, whose members were all elected.

With the Foraker Act of 1900, the U.S. Congress created a new government in Puerto Rico. The United States appointed a governor to be in charge of the island's elected civil government. The Foraker Act also created a legislative assembly made up of two houses: an executive council and a house of delegates. The executive council was made up of eleven members who were appointed by the U.S. president with approval from the U.S. Senate. The thirty-five members of the house of delegates were elected by qualified voters in Puerto Rico.

The Jones Act of 1917 saw the creation of a legislature made up of two chambers: the Senate and the House of Representatives of Puerto Rico. Voting Puerto Ricans were responsible for electing members to both of these chambers. There were nineteen senate members and thirty-nine house members.

In 1948, the U.S. Congress gave Puerto Ricans the right to vote for their own governor. In 1950, President Harry Truman approved the Puerto Rican Commonwealth Bill. The bill allowed Puerto Ricans to vote on whether to remain a colony or become a commonwealth. The majority of residents voted for commonwealth status in 1951. As a result, Puerto Rico residents drafted and approved their own constitution for the first time.

The constitution created a system similar to that of the United States, in which powers are kept separate among three branches of government. The Commonwealth of Puerto Rico remains the form of government in effect today.

The Senate of Puerto Rico is the other chamber of the legislative branch. There are normally twenty-seven senators in this chamber. There are sixteen district members, two for each senatorial district. Like the house, the Senate of Puerto Rico can have at least eleven members at large.

There are four types of legislative sessions: regular, special, extraor-

Puerto Rico's capitol building, also known as El Capitolio, looks like a smaller version of the U.S. Captitol Building. The legislature holds its regular sessions inside.

dinary, and special interrogatory. Regular sessions are held twice a year. If it is a general election year, only one regular session is held. If the governor wants the legislative branch to consider a specific matter, he or she will call for a special session. An extraordinary session is used to hear a special message from the governor. In a special interrogatory session, directors of government agencies and public corporations are required to share information about their performance.

There are four parliamentary officials in the legislative branch. The president, or speaker, serves as the chief executive for administrative affairs. Responsibilities of the speaker include filling an opening when the legislature is not in session, appointing standing and special committees, and signing laws approved by his or her chamber. The vice president/vice speaker serves as a substitute for the speaker in certain instances. Functions of the secretary, or clerk, include preparing the minutes from a session and presiding over sessions in which parliamentary officials are elected. The sergeant at arms is responsible for keeping order in the chambers.

Judicial Branch

The judicial branch upholds the Constitution of the Commonwealth of Puerto Rico. The judicial system is made up of three courts: the supreme court, the court of appeals, and the court of first instance.

The court of first instance is where most cases are first heard. This court includes 253 superior judges and eighty-five municipal judges. Superior judges hold office for a term of twelve years, and municipal judges serve eight-year terms.

The middle court, the court of appeals, hears appeals. This means that the court reviews final verdicts from the court of first instance. There must be a minimum of three judges on a panel to review a final verdict from the court of first instance. The court of appeals is made up of thirty-nine judges. The judges serve for terms of sixteen years.

The Supreme Court of Puerto Rico is the court of last resort. Some of the cases heard here are those that have received a final judgment from the court of appeals. The supreme court is made up of a chief justice and six associate judges. The chief justice makes sure that the courts are running efficiently. The chief justice also assigns judges to the court of first instance and the court of appeals.

Supreme court judges are appointed by the governor with the consent of the Senate of Puerto Rico. Members of Puerto Rico's Supreme Court serve for life until reaching the mandatory retirement age of seventy.

Chapter 4

THE ECONOMY OF PUERTO RICO

The economy of a nation involves the production of goods and services and the purchase and use of these goods and services. It takes a nation's people—its workforce—to produce items and provide services. These goods and services fall into various categories, or industries.

Puerto Rico's economy is somewhat connected to the economy of the United States. As a result, factors that shape the U.S. economy—such as oil prices and interest rates—also affect the island's economy. But this doesn't mean that Puerto Rico's economy is identical to that of the United States.

Compared to the United States, Puerto Rico is not a wealthy place. About 45 percent of the population currently lives below the poverty line. For the last decade, the island's unemployment rate has ranged from 9 to 16 percent. However, when compared to its neighbors in the Caribbean, Puerto Rico's economy is strong. The island's economy also has greatly improved since the 1930s and 1940s.

There are many people in Puerto Rico who are working. In 2007, the island's workforce was estimated at 1.4 million. Of this number, nearly 30 percent held jobs related to services. About 23 percent worked in government jobs, and 20 percent held trade jobs. Nearly 11 percent of the island's labor force was in manufacturing. Slightly

Workers prepare bottles at one of the many pharmaceutical factories found in Puerto Rico.

more than 7 percent of residents worked in construction and mining, and about 4 percent had jobs related to transportation and other public utilities. Less than 4 percent of the labor force held jobs in finance, insurance, and real estate. Jobs in agriculture, which was once Puerto Rico's main industry, made up less than 2 percent of the labor force.

Manufacturing

Although most of Puerto Rico's labor force works in services, it is the manufacturing sector that is responsible for most of the island's gross domestic product (GDP). The GDP is a statistic that measures a nation's economy by looking at all of the goods and services produced by the people and companies within the nation. In recent years, manufacturing has been responsible for 40 to 45 percent of Puerto Rico's GDP.

One example of manufacturing in Puerto Rico is the production of pharmaceutical products and medical devices. The island has been involved in this industry for about forty years. Today, Puerto Rico continues to be a major contributor in the making of medical devices and pharmaceutical products. It manufactures about 50 percent of all pacemakers and defibrillators sold in America. Puerto Rico also makes more than half of the top twenty–selling prescription drugs in the United States. This amounts to 25 percent of the world's biological manufacturing capacity. Given Puerto Rico's starring role in the field of pharmaceuticals, it's no surprise that major pharmaceutical and medical device companies such as Eli Lilly, Wyeth, and Bristol-Myers Squibb have operations on the island. Along with pharmaceuticals, Puerto Rico also manufactures electronics, apparel, and food products.

Each year, cruise ships bring about one million people to Puerto Rico. The Port of San Juan is the second largest cruise port in the Western Hemisphere.

Service

The service sector is the industry with the most workers in Puerto Rico. This sector is made up of workers who help businesses or people or who sell goods. Teachers are considered service workers. Travel agents, tour guides, and hotel staff members are some examples of service workers with jobs in tourism.

Tourism is a vital part of Puerto Rico's service sector. Tourists spend money on food, sightseeing activities, hotels, and more. As a result, tourist activity gives a large boost to Puerto Rico's overall economy. According to the Puerto Rican Tourism Company, an estimated 3.9 million tourists visited the island in 2008. As of 2007, some sixty thousand jobs in Puerto Rico were in tourism.

Imports and Exports

The importing and exporting of goods and services affect a nation's economy. The goods and services made by a nation are either

Puerto Rico's Sugar Industry

While pharmaceuticals play a key part in Puerto Rico's economy today, in the past the sugar industry was the island's economic powerhouse. Sugarcane was first planted on the island in 1516, and by the end of the eighteenth century, it was among the island's principal products.

After the United States gained control of Puerto Rico, the sugar industry really took off. In the early 1900s, the United States eliminated import taxes on items from Puerto Rico. This made Puerto Rican products cheaper for Americans to buy, and demand increased. The United States also gave Puerto Rican–made products the same full tariff protection that American-made items received. Within ten years, the production of sugar in Puerto Rico increased by 331 percent.

The island's sugar industry also prospered with the arrival of U.S. corporations. By the 1930s, about half of the sugar mills in Puerto Rico were owned by U.S. companies. At the height of the industry, Puerto Rico was producing 1.3 million tons of sugar each year.

In the 1950s, however, the sugar industry began to decline. Operation Bootstrap was a key reason for this slowdown. Launched in the 1940s, Operation Bootstrap was a government program designed to shift Puerto Rico away from its dependence on agriculture and toward industrialization. Too often, a hurricane would destroy entire crops and have a negative impact on the island's economy. Operation Bootstrap caused the number of manufacturing jobs to increase.

Eventually, the cost of producing sugar rose in Puerto Rico. Nearby countries were able to offer a less expensive product. In time, the exportation of sugar slowed and mills closed. Today, Puerto Rico is known for the production of pharmaceuticals and medical devices, not sugar. Many more Puerto Rican citizens have manufacturing jobs than have jobs related to agriculture.

purchased and used by its residents or exported (sent) to another nation and sold there. When the goods and services used by residents come from another nation, they are known as imports.

The importing and exporting of goods plays a big part in Puerto Rico's economy. The island imports and exports more than $100 billion in goods each year.

Puerto Rico imports goods worth about $45 billion a year. Due to the island's manufacturing activity, the largest segment of imports is raw materials. These materials are used for production and consumption. Items that Puerto Rico imports include chemicals, clothing, food, fish, machinery and equipment, and petroleum products. Puerto Rico receives most of its imports—about 50 percent—from the United States. About 20 percent comes from Ireland.

Puerto Rico exports goods worth about $60 billion a year. Given the island's involvement in pharmaceuticals, it makes sense that the largest segment of exports is chemicals, including medicines. Puerto Rico also exports apparel, electronics, beverage concentrates, medical equipment, rum, and canned tuna. Nearly 80 percent of the island's exports are sent to the United States. Smaller percentages are sent to European countries, such as the Netherlands, Belgium, and Germany.

Chapter 5

PEOPLE FROM PUERTO RICO:
PAST AND PRESENT

From inspiring politicians to polished performers to sensational sports heroes, the following Puerto Ricans have made a mark on the commonwealth's history.

Ramón Emeterio Betances (1827–1898) Born in 1827, Ramón Emeterio Betances fought for slaves and other Puerto Ricans under Spanish rule to be treated with equality and fairness. He cofounded a secret group aimed at freeing the slaves and was exiled several times for such activities. Betances is best known for inspiring the Grito de Lares uprising. He also helped others as a doctor. Betances set up a hospital on the island and worked to save people from a cholera epidemic.

Roberto Clemente (1934–1972) The youngest of seven children, Roberto Clemente spent his childhood working to earn extra money for his family. He went on to join the Pittsburgh Pirates baseball team and helped lead them to a 1960 World Series win. During his career, Clemente was named National League MVP and World Series MVP. He won four National League batting championships and twelve Gold

During his remarkable career, Angel Cordero Jr. won the Eclipse Award as the nation's best jockey twice. By the time he retired, Cordero had scored more than seven thousand wins.

Glove awards. He also made three thousand hits. Clemente was the first Latin American player to be inducted into the Baseball Hall of Fame.

Angel Cordero Jr. (1942–) Angel Cordero Jr. was a teen when he won his first Puerto Rican horse race. He went on to win the Kentucky Derby—three times. He's had two wins each in the Kentucky Oaks and the Preakness, and he's won at the Belmont and the Arlington Million. In 1991, he became the third jockey to score seven thousand wins. Cordero has been inducted into the National Museum Racing Hall of

Puerto Rico's Taíno Heritage

When Christopher Columbus discovered Puerto Rico, he found out that he was not the first person on the island. The Taíno, an Indian group, had arrived around 700 CE. The name they gave to Puerto Rico was Borikén, or Borinquén according to the Spanish. This name translates to "land of the noble lord."

Throughout the island, the Taínos lived in villages that varied in size. Some villages had a population of about one hundred Taínos, and some villages had a population of thousands. The Taínos lived in round, wooden huts called *bohios* and slept in hammocks. Some of these thatched huts would house as many as forty family members.

For food, the Taínos went hunting and fishing, made bread, and grew crops. They also made pottery, weaved baskets, and created woodcarvings. They were led by a system of chiefs, or caciques. One chief lived in each main village. The chief lived in the biggest hut. Medicine men ranked just below chiefs. They were followed by the subchiefs and, finally, the workers.

When they weren't working, the Taínos would play a soccerlike game on ceremonial ballparks that they had built. Playing the game involved a rubber ball and two teams of ten to thirty players. The Taínos believed that those who won the game were meant to have a fine crop and good health. The ballparks, which featured rows of large stone blocks, were also used for public ceremonies. Archaeologists have found and preserved two examples of these courts.

Today, the Indian population in Puerto Rico is small, but the influence of the Taíno still exists. Some farmers sow certain plants using a Taíno technique. The farmers of today also use the stout double broadswords once used by the Taínos to clear land and sow fields.

The Taíno are also credited with the contribution of maracas, a musical instrument. Words used by the Taíno, such as "maracas" and "iguana," can be heard in Puerto Rican Spanish. A Taíno influence can also be found in traditional Puerto Rican meals. The heavy use of root vegetables is linked to the Taíno way of life.

Fame and the Nassau County Sports Hall of Fame.

Rita Moreno (1931–)
Rita Moreno started out as a dancer. At thirteen, she had her debut on Broadway. A year later, she was in Hollywood. Moreno made it into the *Guinness Book of World Records* when she became the first woman to win all four of the major show business awards. She won the Oscar for the movie *West Side Story*, an Emmy for an appearance on *The Muppet Show*, the Tony for her Broadway performance in *The Ritz*, and a Grammy for her work on *The Electric Company* album. In 2000, she received a Living Legend award from the Library of Congress.

Rita Moreno's career has included award-winning performances on the stage, in television, and in films. A multitalented artist, Moreno has worked as a singer, dancer, and actress.

Luis Muñoz Marín (1898–1980) The son of Luis Muñoz Rivera, Luis Muñoz Marín helped shape Puerto Rico both politically and economically. A designer of both Operation Bootstrap and Operation Serenity, Muñoz Marín also founded the Partido Popular Democrático, a political party that is still in existence. IIe was instrumental in convincing the United States that Puerto Rico was ready to elect its own governor.

In 1948, he became the island's first popularly elected governor. He served for four consecutive four-year terms. As governor, he proposed that Puerto Rico become an associated free state. Eventually, the United States allowed the island to draw up its own constitution as a commonwealth.

Luis Muñoz Rivera (1859–1916) Luis Muñoz Rivera was greatly involved in the movement for Puerto Rico's independence from Spain. He cofounded the Autonomist Party and founded *La Democracia*, a newspaper that served as a voice for the party. In 1897, when Puerto Rico gained independence from Spain, Muñoz Rivera was named secretary of state and chief of the cabinet. In 1910, he was elected resident commissioner to the U.S. Congress, where he pushed for autonomy from America. His efforts resulted in the Jones Act, which gave Puerto Rico's government more autonomy.

Felisa Rincón de Gautier (1897–1994) In the 1930s, Felisa Rincón de Gautier not only supported the right for Puerto Rican women to vote, but she was also one of the first women to vote. Better known as Doña Felisa, Rincón de Gautier was one of the first women to hold a leadership role in a Puerto Rican political party. In 1946, she became the first female mayor of San Juan. She served for twenty-two years. As mayor, Rincón de Gautier brought preschool child-care centers, new schools, and housing projects with nurseries to San Juan. She also organized municipal centers to care for the elderly and a legal aid center to serve the needy.

A trailblazer, Felisa Rincón de Gautier helped pave the way for women to have more political power. Along with being mayor of San Juan, she also served as a U.S. ambassador of goodwill.

Juan "Chi Chi" Rodriguez (1935–) As a poor youngster in the 1940s, Juan "Chi Chi" Rodriguez practiced golfing by using guava branches for clubs and balls made from tin cans. Since then, he has had eight wins on the PGA Tour and twenty-two wins on the Champions Tour. He has also represented Puerto Rico on twelve World Cup teams. He is also a World Golf Hall of Fame inductee. Rodriguez has raised money for the Children's Hospital of Puerto Rico and has given poor children access to the golf course where he was first noticed.

Lola Rodríguez de Tió (1843–1924) Inspired by the Grito de Lares revolt, Lola Rodríguez de Tió penned patriotic lyrics to the tune of "La Borinqueña," Puerto Rico's national anthem. The song was well-liked. She is also known for suggesting that the Puerto Rican flag should look like Cuba's flag, but with the colors reversed. For her revolutionary activities, Rodríguez de Tió was exiled from Puerto Rico several times. In 1876, her first book of poetry was published. Some 2,500 copies were sold.

Sonia Sotomayor (1954–) Born to Puerto Rican parents, Sonia Sotomayor grew up in a Bronx public housing project and went on to become the first Hispanic justice to serve on the U.S. Supreme Court. A graduate of Princeton University and Yale Law School, Sotomayor spent most of her legal career in public service. As a U.S. district court judge for the Southern District of New York, Sotomayor became known for saving baseball. Her ruling led to the end of a strike that had cancelled the 1994 World Series.

Timeline

1493	Christopher Columbus lands in Puerto Rico on November 19. In honor of St. John the Baptist, Columbus names the island San Juan Bautista.
1508	Spanish explorer Juan Ponce de León arrives and sets up the island's first colony in Caparra, an area near San Juan. About a year later, he becomes Puerto Rico's first governor.
1521	The Caparra colony moves to the location of present-day San Juan. Instead of San Juan Bautista, the island is now called Puerto Rico.
1528	The French attempt to take control of the island and fail. They succeed in burning the San Germán colony.
1595	Sir Francis Drake unsuccessfully tries to take control of Puerto Rico in the name of the English.
1598	Led by the Third Earl of Cumberland, the British attack again. They take over San Juan for several months before leaving due to a dysentery outbreak.
1625	The Dutch invade the island and occupy San Juan for about a month. They burn down the city when they retreat.
1797	On their third and last attempt to take over the island, the British fail again.
1868	Grito de Lares occurs on September 23. Puerto Rican protesters briefly take over the town of Lares. Spanish forces stop the revolt.
1873	After years of slave uprisings and struggles, the Spanish National Assembly abolishes slavery on March 22.
1897	Spain grants Puerto Rico autonomy.
1898	The Spanish-American War begins. The war lasts six months and ends with Spain surrendering Puerto Rico to America.
1900	The U.S. Congress passes the Foraker Act, which establishes a civilian government in Puerto Rico that is run by the United States.
1917	President Woodrow Wilson signs the Jones Act, granting U.S. citizenship to Puerto Ricans.

1937	A march for independence in the town of Ponce ends with the deaths of seventeen protestors and two police officers. The March 21 event becomes known as La Masacre de Ponce (the Ponce Massacre).
1948	Luis Muñoz Marín becomes Puerto Rico's first freely elected governor. He serves for sixteen years.
1950s	Operation Bootstrap results in an increase in manufacturing jobs. Operation Serenity, a complement to Operation Bootstrap, promotes the arts.
1952	On July 25, Puerto Rico becomes a U.S. commonwealth. Elections are held every four years.
1967	Puerto Rico holds a vote to see if it should become a U.S. state. More than 60 percent of voters decide it should remain a commonwealth.
1993	Another vote is held regarding U.S. statehood. The majority of Puerto Rican voters choose commonwealth status.
1999	An islander is killed during U.S. military target practice on Vieques. Major protests occur.
2000	Former San Juan mayor Sila Maria Calderón becomes the first woman to be elected governor of Puerto Rico.
2003	Following some sixty years of use of the island, the U.S. military withdraws from Vieques.
2006	For two weeks, government offices and schools are shut down due to a serious budget crisis.
2010	The U.S. House of Representatives passes a measure to give Puerto Rico a new vote regarding commonwealth status.

Commonwealth motto:	*Joannes Est Nomen Eius* ("His Name Is John")
Commonwealth capital:	San Juan
Commonwealth tree:	Ceiba
Commonwealth bird:	Reinita mora (*Spindalis portoricensis*)
Commonwealth flower:	Flor de maga
Commonwealth date:	July 25, 1952
Commonwealth nickname:	La Isla del Encanto ("The Island of Enchantment")
Total area:	5,324 square miles (13,791 sq km)
Population:	Approximately 4,000,000
Length of coastline:	311 miles (501 km)
Highest elevation:	Cerro de Punta, at 4,393 feet (1,339 m)
Lowest elevation:	Sea level, at the Caribbean Sea
Major rivers:	Grande de Arecibo, Grande de Añasco, La Plata, Cibuco, Grande de Loíza, Bayamón
Major lake:	Laguna Tortuguero

Flag of Puerto Rico

Seal of Puerto Rico

Deepest gorge:	San Cristóbal Canyon, which has walls up to 700 feet (210 m) high
Highest waterfall:	Río Usabón, which plummets 500 feet (153 m)
Hottest temperature recorded in the capital:	98°F (36°C) in San Juan, October 9, 1981
Coldest temperature recorded in the capital:	60°F (15°C) in San Juan, March 3, 1957
Origin of commonwealth name:	Ponce de León gave the name Puerto Rico, which which means "rich port," to the city now known as San Juan. It later became the name of the entire island.
Chief agricultural products:	Sugarcane, coffee, pineapples, plantains, bananas
Major industries:	Pharmaceuticals, electronics, apparel, food products, tourism
Political parties:	National Democratic Party, National Republican Party of Puerto Rico, New Progressive Party (PNP), Popular Democratic Party (PPD), Puerto Rican Independence Party (PIP)

Reinita mora

Flor de maga

GLOSSARY

autonomy The self-government of a state, community, or group.

bicameral Made up of two different and separate lawmaking chambers or branches.

bioluminescence The production of visible light by living organisms.

cay A small, low island made up of coral or sand.

cholera An infectious disease of the small intestine that comes on quickly and is severe. Symptoms include diarrhea, dehydration, vomiting, and muscle cramps.

dysentery A disease of the lower intestinal tract. Symptoms include inflammation, severe diarrhea, fever, and the passing of blood and mucus.

epidemic An outbreak of a disease that spreads rapidly by infection and affects many people at the same time.

estuary The part of a river where its current meets the tides and freshwater mixes with saltwater.

galleon A large sailing ship with three masts and a square rig. Such ships were typically used from the fifteenth to the nineteenth centuries, especially by the Spanish.

islet A small island.

karst A landscape of limestone where erosion has caused sinkholes, caverns, underground streams, and long, narrow cracks.

limestone A sedimentary rock that is mainly made up of calcium carbonate. The rock is formed from the skeletons and shells of marine organisms.

manatee A large, aquatic mammal found in warm, coastal waters. It eats plants and has front flippers and a flattened tail.

microorganism An extremely small organism, such as a virus or bacterium, that can only be seen under a microscope.

petroglyph A line drawing or carving found on rock that has typically been created during prehistoric times.

republic A political system that allows people to elect representatives and officers who are responsible to them.

stalactite A mineral deposit in the shape of an icicle that hangs from the roof of a cave. It is formed by the dripping of mineral-rich water, which seeps into the cave's roof from the ground above.

stalagmite A cone-shaped mineral deposit that is attached to the floor of a cave. It is formed by mineral-rich water that drips from the roof of a cave and lands on the cave's floor.

Comité Noviembre

Puerto Rican Heritage Month Fiscal Agency
Institute for the Puerto Rican/Hispanic Elderly
105 East 22nd Street
New York, NY 10010
(212) 677-4181
Web site: http://www.comitenoviembre.org
Established in 1987, the organization plans and promotes annual programs and events that deal with all areas of Puerto Rican life.

National Geographic Society

1145 17th Street NW
Washington, DC 20036-4688
(800) 647-5463
Web site: http://www.kids.nationalgeographic.com
National Geographic produces a Web site and magazine that focus on people, places, and creatures from around the world.

Puerto Rican Endowment for the Humanities

P.O. Box 9023920
San Juan, PR 00902-3920
(787) 721-2087
Web site: http://www.fphpr.org/sobre_nosotros/nuestra_institucion.asp
This is a nonprofit organization that sponsors various programs aimed at benefiting Puerto Ricans and promoting the island's culture.

Puerto Rico Federal Affairs Administration

1100 17th Street NW, Suite 800
Washington, DC 20036
(202) 778-0710
Web site: http://www.prfaa.com/prfaa.asp
The administration's Washington, D.C., office serves as a link between the government

officials of Puerto Rico and the U.S. federal government. The site offers information about the current governor's policies for the island.

United Confederation of Taíno People

Roberto Múkaro Agueibana Borrero, President UCTP-OIRRC

P.O. Box 4515, Grand Central Station

New York, NY10163

(212) 604-4186

Web site: http://www.uctp.org

This organization promotes and protects the culture, rights, and traditions of the Taíno and other people originating from the Caribbean.

El Yunque National Forest

HC-01, Box 13490

Rio Grande, PR 00745-9625

(787) 888-1880

Web site: http://www.fs.fed.us/r8/caribbean/index.shtml

Through its Web site, El Yunque National Forest offers a range of information related to the rainforest, including maps and publications, as well as a kids' page with plant and wildlife facts.

Web Sites

Due to the changing nature of Internet links, Rosen Publishing has developed an online list of Web sites related to the subject of this book. This site is updated regularly. Please use this link to access the list:

http://www.rosenlinks.com/uspp/prpp

FOR FURTHER READING

Bjorklund, Ruth. *Puerto Rico* (It's My State). New York, NY: Marshall Cavendish Benchmark, 2007.

Cofer, Judith Ortiz. *Call Me Maria: A Novel*. New York, NY: Orchard Books, 2004.

Conley, Kate A. *The Puerto Rican Americans* (Immigrants in America). San Diego, CA: Lucent Books, 2005.

Fein, Eric. *How to Draw Puerto Rico's Sights and Symbols* (A Kid's Guide to Drawing America). New York, NY: PowerKids Press, 2002.

Gutner, Howard. *Puerto Rico* (True Book). New York, NY: Children's Press, 2009.

Heinrichs, Ann. *Puerto Rico* (Welcome to the U.S.A.). Chanhassen, MN: Child's World, 2005.

Jaffe, Nina. *The Golden Flower: A Taíno Myth from Puerto Rico*. Houston, TX: Piñata Books, 2005.

Levy, Patricia, and Nazry Bahrawi. *Puerto Rico* (Cultures of the World). New York, NY: Marshall Cavendish Benchmark, 2006.

Lopez, Jose Javier. *Puerto Rico* (Modern World Nations). Philadelphia, PA: Chelsea House, 2006.

Marcovitz, Hal. *Puerto Ricans* (Successful Americans). Philadelphia, PA: Mason Crest Publishers, 2009.

Márquez, Herón. *Roberto Clemente: Baseball's Humanitarian Hero* (Trailblazer Biography). Minneapolis, MN: Carolrhoda Books, 2005.

Ostow, Micol. *Emily Goldberg Learns to Salsa*. New York, NY: Razorbill, 2007.

Petrillo, Valerie. *A Kid's Guide to Latino History: More Than 50 Activities*. Chicago, IL: Chicago Review Press, 2009.

Polikoff, Barbara Garland. *Why Does the Coquí Sing?* New York, NY: Holiday House, 2004.

Stafford, Jim. *Puerto Ricans' History and Promise: Americans Who Cannot Vote* (Hispanic Heritage). Philadelphia, PA: Mason Crest Publishers, 2006.

Stille, Darlene R. *Puerto Rico* (America the Beautiful). New York, NY: Children's Press, 2009.

Tagliaferro, Linda. *Puerto Rico in Pictures* (Visual Geography Series). Minneapolis, MN: Lerner Publications, 2004.

Taus-Bolstad, Stacy. *Puerto Ricans in America* (In America). Minneapolis, MN: Lerner Publications, 2005.

Worth, Richard. *Puerto Rico in American History* (From Many Cultures, One History). Berkeley Heights, NJ: Enslow Publishers, 2008.

BIBLIOGRAPHY

Albanese, Marta S. E-mail message to author, June 22, 2009.

Associated Press. "Cost, Competition Decay Puerto Rico's Sugar Industry." Puerto Rico-Herald.org, 2000. Retrieved June 11, 2009 (http://www.puertorico-herald.org/issues/vol4n06/SugarIndusDown-en.html).

Associated Press. "Supplies Rushed to Puerto Rico." *New York Times*, September 22, 1989. Retrieved June 11, 2009 (http://www.nytimes.com/1989/09/22/US/supplies-rushed-to-puerto-rico.html?pagewanted-1).

Ayala, César J., and Rafael Bernabe. *Puerto Rico in the American Century: A History Since 1898*. Chapel Hill, NC: University of North Carolina Press, 2007.

Balletto, Barbara, ed. *Insight Guide Puerto Rico* (Insight Guides). Long Island City, NY: Langenscheidt, 2007.

Casiano Communications, Inc. "The Puerto Rico Investor's Guide to Government Resources." Government Development Bank for Puerto Rico, 2007. Retrieved June 8, 2009 (http://www.gdbpr.com/publications-reports/cb-investors.html).

Domenech, Francisco J., and Maritza Torres–Rivera. "Legislative Process in Puerto Rico." Office of Legislative Services to the Puerto Rico Legislative Assembly, August 8, 2007. Retrieved June 10, 2009 (http://www.oslpr.org/english/master.asp?NAV = MEDIA-PRESENT).

Edmondson, Jolee. "There's Only One Chi Chi." Golf.com, 2009. Retrieved June 7, 2009 (http://www.golf.com/golf/advertisers/dow/humanside/profiles/c_rodriguez.htm).

Fundación Felisa Rincón de Gautier, Inc. "Doña Felisa Rincón de Gautier." 2008. Retrieved June 17, 2009 (http://www.museofelisarincon.com/english.htm).

Gobierno de Puerto Rico: Official Web Site of the Government of Puerto Rico. "Ramas Gubernamentales (Government Branches)." Retrieved June 10, 2009 (http://www.gobierno.pr/GPRPortal/Inicio/RamasGubernamentales).

Government Development Bank for Puerto Rico. "Current Economic Briefing." 2008. Retrieved June 10, 2009 (http://www.gdbpr.com/economy/introduction_economy.html).

Kelly, Martin. "Spanish American War Essentials." About.com. Retrieved June 10, 2009 (http://americanhistory.about.com/od/spanishamwar/tp/spanish-american-war.htm).

Library of Congress. "Hispanic Americans in Congress—Luis Muñoz Rivera." Retrieved June 12, 2009 (http://www.loc.gov/rr/hispanic/congress/munozrivera.html).

Library of Congress. "Lola Rodríguez de Tió." Retrieved June 12, 2009 (http://www.loc.gov/rr/hispanic/1898/lola.html).

Library of Congress. "Ramón Emeterio Betances." Retrieved June 12, 2009 (http://www.loc.gov/rr/hispanic/1898/betances.html).

Library of Congress. "Rita Moreno." Retrieved June 17, 2009 (http://www.loc.gov/about/awardshonors/livinglegends/bio/morenor.html).

National Thoroughbred Racing Association. "Angel Cordero Jr.—NTRA." Retrieved June 11, 2009 (http://www.ntra.com/stats_bios.aspx?id=1774).

National Weather Service Forecast Office: San Juan, PR. "National Weather Service Climate." Retrieved November 9, 2009 (http://www.weather.gov/climate/xmacis.php?wfo=sju).

New Deal Network. "Puerto Rico in the Great Depression." Retrieved June 10, 2009 (http://newdeal.feri.org/search_details.cfm?link=http://newdeal.feri.org/pr/pr06.htm).

New York Times. "Sonia Sotomayor News—The *New York Times*: Overview." August 6, 2009. Retrieved February 22, 2010 (http://topics.nytimes.com/top/reference/timestopics/people/s/sonia_sotomayor/index.html).

Office of Legislative Services to the Puerto Rico Legislative Assembly. "The Constitution of the Commonwealth of Puerto Rico." Retrieved June 10, 2009 (http://oslpr.org/english/master.asp?NAV=LEYES).

Office of Legislative Services to the Puerto Rico Legislative Assembly. "The Judiciary Act of the Commonwealth of Puerto Rico." Retrieved June 10, 2009 (http://oslpr.org/english/master.asp?NAV=LEYES).

Pace, Eric. "Felisa Rincón de Gautier, 97, Mayor of San Juan." *New York Times*, September 19, 1994. Retrieved June 17, 2009 (http://www.nytimes.com/1994/09/19/obituaries/felisa-rincon-de-gautier-97-mayor-of-san-juan.html).

PBS.org. "Rita Moreno Bio." March 2005. Retrieved June 11, 2009 (http://www.pbs.org/weta/fridakahlo/about/moreno.html).

PGATour.com. "Tournament Dedicated to Chi Chi Rodriguez." January 14, 2008. Retrieved June 7, 2009 (http://www.pgatour.com/2008/tournaments/r483/01/14/pro_chichi/index.html).

Powell, Albrecht. "Roberto Clemente—Biography of Baseball Legend Roberto Clemente – No. 21 Pittsburgh Pirates." About.com. Retrieved June 11, 2009 (http://pittsburgh.about.com/od/pirates/p/clemente.htm).

Sainsbury, Brendan, and Nate Cavalieri. *Puerto Rico.* 4th ed. Footscray, Victoria, Australia; London, England: Lonely Planet, 2008.

U.S. Fish and Wildlife Service. "Vieques National Wildlife Refuge." Retrieved June 11, 2009 (http://www.fws.gov/caribbean/Refuges/Vieques).

INDEX

About the Author

Maria DaSilva-Gordon used her passion for travel as inspiration for this book. In addition to traveling in the United States, she has traveled to Laos, Cambodia, Thailand, Australia, New Zealand, and sixteen European countries on her own. When not traveling, she spends her time writing for newspapers, trade publications, and the occasional Web site. She also teaches journalism workshops to students of various learning abilities and grade levels through her business, Making Headlines, LLC.

Photo Credits

Cover (top left) B. Anthony Stewart/National Geographic/Getty Images; cover (top right, bottom) Hola Images/Getty Images; pp. 3, 6, 14, 20, 25, 30, 37 © www.istockphoto.com/Marta Lugo; p. 4 (top) www.lib.utexas.edu/maps/puerto_rico.html; pp. 7, 11, 18 © AP Images; p. 12 © Pryor Maresa/Animals Animals-Earth Scenes; p. 13 Shutterstock.com; p. 15 Robert Frerck/Stone/Getty Images; p. 19 Gordon Parks/Time & Life Pictures/Getty Images; pp. 21, 23 © www.istockphoto.com/TexPhoto; p. 26 © David R. Frazier Photolibrary, Inc./Alamy; p. 27 © Cameron Davidson/Alamy; p. 29 Glowimages/Getty Images; p. 31 Robert Riger/Getty Images; p. 33 Hulton Archive/Getty Images; p. 35 Donald Uhrbrock/Time & Life Pictures/Getty Images; p. 39 (left) Courtesy of Robesus, Inc.; p. 40 (left) © www.istockphoto.com/Matthew Ragen.

Designer: Les Kanturek; Editor: Andrea Sclarow;
Photo Researcher: Amy Feinberg